CLASSIC HYMNS & REFLECTIONS
ON OUR SAVIOUR

JESUS
THE GIFT OF
Hope

INTRODUCTION BY TWILA PARIS
DEVOTIONS BY KEN ABRAHAM
ART & DESIGN BY LARRY LAWSON

THE
CARABLE
GROUP
An Association of Christian Retailers

ISBN: 0-87162-672-1

WARNER PRESS, INC.
PRINTED IN MEXICO

Throughout centuries of Christianity, hymns have endured as irreplaceable and powerful elements of worship that lead us into God's presence, and greater obedience to Him. Many of these hymns center around our beloved Saviour, His wonderful love for us, and the blessed hope that we have through Him.

As you read these lyrics and reflections on some of our greatest hymns about Jesus, may your own walk with God be made richer, and may you be inspired again to lift your voice in worship as the hope of Christ fills your heart!

TWILA PARIS

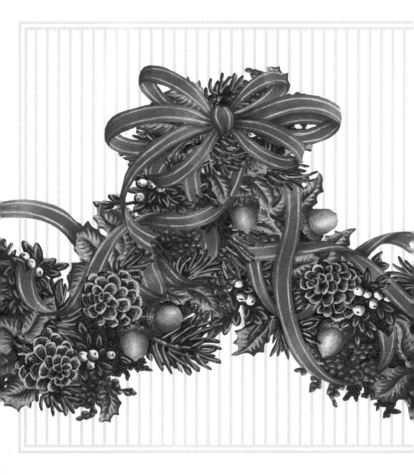

HIS
CRUCIFIXION

O SACRED HEAD, NOW WOUNDED

WHEN I SURVEY THE WONDROUS CROSS

O Sacred Head, Now Wounded
PAUL GERHARDT

O sacred Head, now wounded,
With grief and shame weighed down,
Now scornfully surrounded
With thorns, Thy only crown,
How art Thou pale with anguish,
With sore abuse and scorn!
How does that visage languish
Which once was bright as morn!

God on a cross? Unthinkable!
Yet there He was ... nails in His hands,
a spear piercing His side, a crown of thorns
on His head. Jesus had never sinned. He had
never said an evil word or done an evil deed,
yet He was dying for those of us who have.
His suffering and death purchased our salvation.
He took our place; He paid the price for our sins.

"Surely our griefs He Himself bore, And our
sorrows He carried.... He was pierced through for our
transgressions, He was crushed for our iniquities;
The chastening for our well-being fell upon Him,
And by His scourging we are healed."

ISAIAH 53:4, 5

When I Survey the Wondrous Cross

ISAAC WATTS

When I survey the wondrous cross
On which the Prince of glory died,
My richest gain I count but loss,
And pour contempt on all my pride.

The world wants Jesus without the cross,
but where Christ is, there is always a cross …
not just His, but ours. The cross of Jesus Christ
demands a response … not simply an acceptance,
or an acknowledgement, but a total
commitment of our lives to the One who
died upon it, and yet now lives.

"He died for all, that they who live should
no longer live for themselves, but for Him who
died and rose again on their behalf."

2 CORINTHIANS 5 : 15

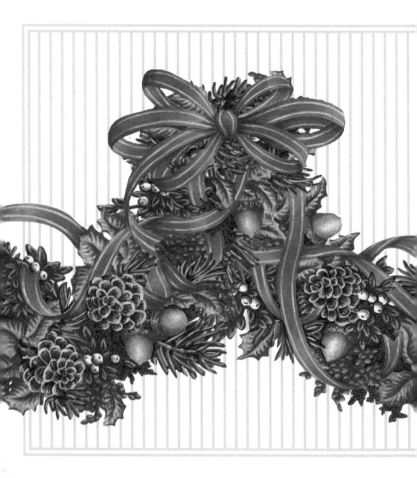

HIS
RESURRECTION
& RETURN

CHRIST THE LORD IS RISEN TODAY

THE SOLID ROCK

COME, THOU ALMIGHTY KING

Christ the Lord Is Risen Today

CHARLES WESLEY

Christ the Lord is risen today,
Alleluia!
Sons of men and angels say:
Alleluia!
Raise your joys and triumphs high,
Alleluia!
Sing, ye heavens, and earth reply:
Alleluia!

The resurrection of Jesus Christ
is a pivotal event in history, and it is
the cornerstone upon which our faith is built.
It separates Christianity from mere religion.
Because we know Jesus is alive, death, the grave,
and hell have no power over us.
Life becomes an adventure.
If God can raise Jesus from the dead,
He can do anything!

"If Christ has not been raised,
your faith is worthless; you are still in your sins....
But now Christ has been raised from the dead,
the first fruits of those who are asleep."

1 CORINTHIANS 15:17, 20

The Solid Rock

EDWARD MOTE

My hope is built on nothing less
Than Jesus' blood and righteousness;
I dare not trust the sweetest frame,
But wholly lean on Jesus' name.
On Christ, the solid Rock, I stand;
All other ground is sinking sand,
All other ground is sinking sand.

Where do your hope and security lie?
In your profession, your home, bank accounts,
abilities, material possessions, other people?
Only Jesus can satisfy the longings of your soul.
In Him, we have a hope that will not pass away.
He is our hope in this world, and He makes
certain our hope in heaven to come.

"Blessed be the God and Father of our Lord Jesus Christ,
who according to His great mercy has caused us to be
born again to a living hope through the resurrection of
Jesus Christ from the dead, to obtain an inheritance which
is imperishable ... reserved in heaven for you."

1 PETER 1:3, 4

Come, Thou Almighty King

ANONYMOUS

Come, Thou Almighty King,
Help us Thy name to sing,
Help us to praise:
Father, all-glorious,
O'er all victorious,
Come, and reign over us,
Ancient of Days.

The blessed hope of Christians is that one day
soon our Lord Jesus will return to rule eternally.
In the meantime, Christ comes to us
by His Holy Spirit to rule our lives internally.
As we look forward to His Second Coming,
we can experience the Spirit of Jesus right now.
We can have Christ's presence in our lives on
a daily basis. Even so, Lord Jesus, come!

"May the Lord cause you to increase and abound
in love for one another ... so that He may establish
your hearts unblamable in holiness before our God
and Father at the coming of our Lord Jesus
with all His saints."

1 THESSALONIANS 3:12, 13

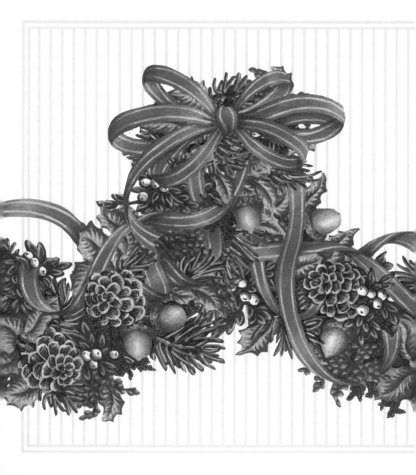

HIS REIGN & LORDSHIP

ALL HAIL THE POWER OF JESUS' NAME

FAIREST LORD JESUS

All Hail the Power of Jesus' Name
EDWARD PERRONET

All hail the power of Jesus' name!
Let angels prostrate fall;
Bring forth the royal diadem,
And crown Him Lord of all;
Bring forth the royal diadem,
And crown Him Lord of all!

Jesus Christ is Lord and King, not just one of these days, but right now! One day soon, however, all of creation will acknowledge Jesus as Master. It is not a question of *if* the world will bow before Him; the only question is *when*. The ultimate encounter of our lives will be the moment we see Jesus face to face.

"God highly exalted Him, and bestowed on Him the name which is above every name, that at the name of Jesus every knee should bow, of those who are in heaven, and on earth, and under the earth, and that every tongue should confess that Jesus Christ is Lord, to the glory of God the Father."

PHILIPPIANS 2:9-11

Fairest Lord Jesus

ANONYMOUS

Fairest Lord Jesus,
Ruler of all nature,
O Thou of God and man the Son:
Thee will I cherish,
Thee will I honor,
Thou my soul's glory, joy, and crown.

As we sing *Fairest Lord Jesus*, we are tempted to
think of Jesus as a weak, timid type of Master.
A glance at the lyrics, however, and an
understanding of Scripture will quickly
reveal that He is "fair" in the sense that He is
beautiful, impartial, free from any imperfections.
Nothing or no one can compare to Him.
He is worthy of our praise and honor.

"Worthy is the Lamb that was slain
to receive power and riches and wisdom
and might and honor and glory and blessing."
REVELATION 5:12

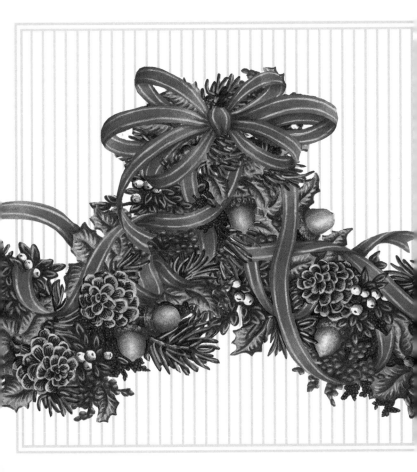

HIS LIFE
IN OUR LIVES

SAVIOR, LIKE A SHEPHERD LEAD US

MY JESUS, I LOVE THEE

'TIS SO SWEET TO TRUST IN JESUS

Savior, Like a Shepherd Lead Us

DOROTHY A. THRUPP

Savior, like a Shepherd lead us,
Much we need Thy tender care;
In Thy pleasant pastures feed us;
For our use Thy folds prepare.
Blessed Jesus, Blessed Jesus,
Thou hast bought us, Thine we are;
Blessed Jesus, Blessed Jesus,
Thou hast bought us, Thine we are.

A great mystery of God is that He does not force us to follow Him, but gently leads us in the path in which we should go. As we obey His commands, He continues to expand our horizons, to illumine our minds with ideas and insights, and to open us to vistas of spiritual possibilities we had not imagined before. Can we take another path? Yes ... but who would want to?

"Trust in the Lord with all your heart, And do not lean on your own understanding. In all your ways acknowledge Him, And He will make your paths straight."

PROVERBS 3 : 5 , 6

My Jesus, I Love Thee

WILLIAM R. FEATHERSTONE

My Jesus, I love Thee,
I know Thou art mine;
For Thee all the follies of sin I resign;
My gracious Redeemer,
my Savior art Thou:
If ever I loved Thee, my Jesus, 'tis now.

A strong, motivating factor in our lives should be an attitude of gratitude. The reason we live for Jesus Christ is not because we are afraid of eternal damnation … nor is it gifts, blessings, or success in this world. It is not even for the reward of heaven. We live for Jesus because we love Him. After the pain and humiliation He suffered on the cross, we *owe* Him our lives.

"Fixing our eyes on Jesus, the author and perfecter of faith, who for the joy set before Him endured the cross, despising the shame, and has sat down at the right hand of the throne of God."

HEBREWS 12:2

'Tis So Sweet to Trust in Jesus

LOUISA M. R. STEAD

'Tis so sweet to trust in Jesus,
Just to take Him at His word,
Just to rest upon His promise,
Just to know, "Thus saith the Lord."
Jesus, Jesus, how I trust Him!
How I've proved Him o'er and o'er!
Jesus, Jesus, precious Jesus!
O for grace to trust Him more!

Trusting Jesus is not a goal to be
achieved; it is an exciting journey of faith.
It is a never-ending process. You can never plumb
the depths of God's love. You will never exhaust
His fresh supply of resources in your life.
There is no height, nor depth, no limit at all
to how deeply you can grow in Christ. As you
surrender yourself to Him, and trust Him
for His best in your life, rest assured,
there is more … much more!

"Delight yourself in the Lord; And He will give you
the desires of your heart. Commit your way to the Lord,
Trust also in Him, and He will do it."

PSALM 37:4, 5

"Now the God of peace,
who brought up from the dead
the great Shepherd of the sheep through
the blood of the eternal covenant,
even Jesus our Lord, equip you
in every good thing to do His will,
working in us that which is pleasing
in His sight, through Jesus Christ,
to whom be the glory forever and ever.
Amen."

HEBREWS 13:20, 21